The Netherlands

The Netherlands

BY MARTIN HINTZ

Enchantment of the World™
Second Series

CHILDREN'S PRESS®

An Imprint of Scholastic Inc.

Frontispiece: **Building in Amsterdam**

Consultant: Jeroen Dewulf, Director, Institute of European Studies, University of
California–Berkeley
Please note: All statistics are as up-to-date as possible at the time of publication.

Book production by The Design Lab

Library of Congress Cataloging-in-Publication Data
Hintz, Martin.
  The Netherlands / by Martin Hintz.
      pages cm. — (Enchantment of the world)
  Includes bibliographical references and index.
  Audience: Grades 4–6.
  ISBN 978-0-531-21697-2 (library binding : alk. paper)
1. Netherlands—Juvenile literature. I. Title.
  DJ18.H56 2015
  949.2—dc23   2014047372

1 2 3 4 5 6 7 8 9 10 R 25 24 23 22 21 20 19 18 17 16

Tulip field

Contents

Left to right: **Family, ice-skating, eating herring, harvesting tulips, fields on reclaimed land**

CHAPTER 1

Welcome to the Netherlands!

CANALS CURVING BETWEEN NARROW BUILDINGS IN the old city of Amsterdam. Countless fields of brilliant tulips in bloom. Dozens of bicyclists waiting patiently for a light to turn green so they can be on their way. A bustling port where cranes are loading giant containers onto even larger ships to be sent across the sea.

These are common images of the Netherlands, but the country is much more as well. It is modern and vibrant, full of people from all corners of the world.

The Netherlands is a small country in the northwest of Europe. People sometimes call the Netherlands Holland, but "Holland," in fact, refers only to the Netherlands' western provinces of South Holland and North Holland. Using the incorrect term can by annoying to Dutch people who live in other parts of the country. It's like calling a Welsh person English instead of British.

Opposite: **Bicycles parked next to a canal in Amsterdam. The Netherlands has the highest rate of bicycle ownership in the world.**

The word *Dutch* originated in the Middle Ages, from the Germanic root "dutsch" or "deutsch." It originally meant speakers of High and Low German, two dialects of basic German. But by the end of the 1500s, "Dutch" had become commonly used for the people who lived in the area that is now the Netherlands.

Humans have resided in this flat, low-lying countryside for thousands of years. Much of the land is below sea level, so the people who settled there had to deal with constant flooding.

Twenty centuries ago, the Romans conquered the region. The Romans spoke Latin, and they called the region *terra inferior*, meaning "Low Countries." Originally, this territory included today's Belgium and Luxembourg, but over the years there were many wars and the borders shifted. By the 1400s,

Roman soldiers (in red) fight less well-equipped northern Europeans.

The Kingdom of the Netherlands

The Netherlands is a kingdom officially under the rule of the head of state King Willem-Alexander. The kingdom also incorporates several islands in the Caribbean, including Aruba, Bonaire, Curaçao, Saba, Sint Eustatius, and Sint Maarten. These were once colonies but now enjoy separate political status within the kingdom.

Curaçao is an island near the coast of South America that is part of the Kingdom of the Netherlands. The island features typical Dutch architecture.

the king of Spain claimed control of the Low Countries. Orange became the official color of the Netherlands because patriots from the House of Orange led the Dutch revolt against Spain in the 1500s. After many revolts, battles, and

Cranes load giant containers onto a ship in Rotterdam. Each container is about the size of a school bus.

agreements, the Low Countries eventually split into three parts: the Netherlands, Belgium, and Luxembourg.

The Dutch have long been hardy and resourceful. They needed to push back the sea to increase the amount of land to farm and to expand their cities. They were also eager to move beyond their borders. They traveled to the far corners of the world to establish colonies. The flow of trade that resulted from these expeditions made the Netherlands a wealthy nation. Today, the Netherlands remains a center of international trade and is home to Rotterdam, one of the world's largest ports.

Each July, the people of Amsterdam hold the Keti Koti parade, which commemorates the end of slavery in the Dutch colonies. The Dutch banned slavery in its Caribbean colonies of Suriname and the Antilles in 1863.

Because the Dutch were familiar with many cultures, they were generally open to new ideas. The Dutch often adapted the best of what they found elsewhere and made it their own, whether it was art, food, or political ideas. Many refugees from economic and political turmoil have found a safe haven in the Netherlands. Each group added enormously to the culture that is the Netherlands.

Arts and culture thrive in the Netherlands. Nederlands Dans Theater, based in The Hague, is one of world's leading contemporary dance companies.

This openness has made the Netherlands a vibrant place. Its creative artists and writers have influenced the world's culture for generations. Dutch scientists are internationally renowned. In fact, nineteen Dutch citizens have been awarded the prestigious Nobel Prize, primarily in physics and chemistry. The Dutch people's appreciation of this mix of openness, innovation, and resourcefulness helps make their country unique.

CHAPTER 2

Water, Water Everywhere

THE NETHERLANDS IS A SMALL COUNTRY, COVERING only about 16,033 square miles (41,525 square kilometers), making it barely as large as the U.S. state of New Jersey. The country's southern neighbor is Belgium, while Germany lies to the east. The North Sea, an arm of the Atlantic Ocean, lies to the northwest.

The Dutch people literally created their own country. About 25 percent of the land area in the Netherlands is below sea level, and 50 percent is less than 3 feet (1 meter) above sea level.

Near the Sea

Tens of thousands of years ago, the weight and movement of massive ice sheets called glaciers helped shape the Netherlands. When the ice retreated, it left behind vast boggy stretches. The soil around Amsterdam is still settling, sinking

Opposite: **The ocean is an important part of the landscape in the Netherlands. No point in the country is more than 95 miles (150 km) from the sea.**

The Netherlands' Geographical Features

Area: 16,033 square miles (41,525 sq km)

Highest Elevation: Vaalserberg, 1,053 feet (321 m) above sea level

Lowest Elevation: Prins Alexanderpolder, 22 feet (7 m) below sea level

Length of Coastline: 280 miles (450 km)

Average Daily High Temperature: In Amsterdam, 42°F (6°C) in January, 72°F (22°C) in July

Average Daily Low Temperature: In Amsterdam, 33°F (1°C) in January, 54°F (12°C) in July

Average Annual Rainfall: 33 inches (84 cm)

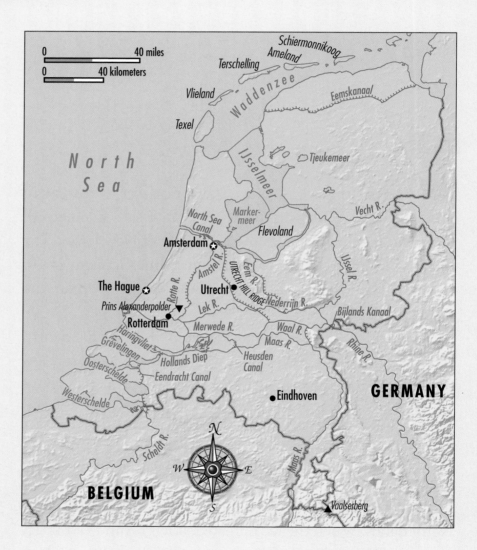

about 1 inch (2 centimeters) per century. Another challenge in keeping the Netherlands dry is the rising ocean. As the world's climate is warming, so much ice in the polar regions is melting that it is causing sea levels to rise about 6 inches (15 cm) each century. The people of the Netherlands have no choice but to deal with the rising seas.

The Netherlands has three distinct physical regions. Along the North Sea coast are dunes and grassy ridges. Ocean currents built long ridges of sand dunes along the coast, and for centuries these dunes protected the land. Eventually,

Gentle dunes cover part of the coastline in the Netherlands.

High and Low

Prins Alexanderpolder, northeast of Rotterdam, is the lowest part of the Netherlands. The city lies 22 feet (7 m) below what is termed the Normal Amsterdam Level (NAP). The top of a huge bolt embedded in a wall of the Muziektheater, Amsterdam's music theater, is used to indicate the standard level in comparing heights. Using this mark, the highest point in the country is 1,053 feet (321 m) above the NAP, at Vaalserberg in the south. This is the point where the Netherlands, Germany, and Belgium come together.

however, the water broke through these natural barriers, flooding far inland. Much of what remains of those early dunes is part of Zuid-Kennemerland National Park.

Sheep graze on the reclaimed land in a polder.

Reclaiming Land

Farther inland are low tracts of land called *polders*, which were reclaimed from the sea. As early as the twelfth century, the people of the Netherlands built long embankments called dikes to halt flooding and create the polders. They used windmills to pump water into the North Sea, leaving behind the fertile polders. There are about 350 miles (560 km) of dikes in the Netherlands. Today, these technological marvels have built-in sensors to report changes in how the dike is holding up in a storm. Massive floodgates on the dikes can be opened during good weather, allowing salt water to enter natural preserves that protect the Netherlands' rare plants and animals. The floodgates are closed during storms. Without this system, land with elevations between 5 feet (1.5 m) below sea level and 5 feet (1.5 m) above sea level would flood twice a day, at high tide. About 60 percent of the Dutch now live on land that was once subject to daily flooding.

North Sea

Afsluitdijk (completed 1932)

Houtribdijk (completed 1975)

Zuiderzee

GERMANY

BELGIUM

Land Reclamation

- Land area prior to the 14th century
- Land reclaimed in the 14th and 15th centuries
- Land reclaimed in the 16th and 17th centuries
- Land reclaimed in the 18th and 19th centuries
- Land reclaimed in the 20th century

A narrow slice of higher ground lies beyond the polders. Crisscrossed by numerous rivers, this fertile land is home to fragrant orchards and thick forests.

Holding Back the Water

There is an old tale of a little Dutch boy who stuck his finger into a hole in a leaking dike and saved the Netherlands. But, of course, holding back the water is not as easy as that. Because most of the country is at or below sea level, finding a safe place to flee if a dike broke would be difficult. Flevoland is the largest polder, nearly three times the size of the island of Manhattan in New York, but it would take just forty-eight hours for it to be submerged if a dike broke there. Catastrophic floods killed tens of thousands of people in 1287, 1404, 1421, 1570, and again 1916. More recently, more than 1,800 people died in flooding in 1953. With this in mind, the government's Ministry of Infrastructure and the Environment manages the country's intricate system of waterways, floodgates, pumping stations, and dikes. As the Dutch say, "Live with the water. But always be prepared!"

Rivers, Canals, and Lakes

A web of rivers crisscrosses the Netherlands. The Maas, Scheldt, and Rhine Rivers are among the most important. Looking for better ways to utilize their inland waters, the Dutch built many canals to make it easier to transport goods. The North Sea Canal is a passage that connects Amsterdam to the North Sea at IJmuiden. The canal was constructed between 1865 and 1876 to enable oceangoing ships to reach the Netherlands' capital. Other major canals include the Heusden, the Bijlands Kanaal, and the Eendracht.

The Netherlands also has many large lakes. The Zuiderzee was once an inlet of the North Sea. In 1932, engineers finalized a dike 19 miles (30 km) long, with a freeway along the top to connect the provinces of North Holland and Friesland. This created an extensive inland lake called the IJsselmeer, which added 626 square miles (1,620 sq km) to the Netherlands' territory.

Dams, dikes, and other barriers protect the Netherlands from the sea.

Climate

In the Netherlands, the weather is generally mild and damp. There is not much frost or snow during the winter, but heavy fog regularly blankets the landscape. Summers are pleasant, with sunny skies. However, the Dutch have learned to carry umbrellas or wear raincoats when they are out walking, because there are often sudden rain showers. In Amsterdam, summer temperatures reach an average high of 72 degrees Fahrenheit (22 degrees Celsius), while in the winter, temperatures rise to only about 42°F (6°C). The average annual precipitation in Amsterdam is 33 inches (84 cm).

A foggy morning in the Netherlands. Fog is common across the country, with Amsterdam experiencing fog an average of 219 days per year.

A Look at Dutch Cities

The largest city in the Netherlands is the capital city of Amsterdam (right), which has a population of about 800,000. Although Amsterdam is the capital, it is not the seat of government. The parliament, the Supreme Court, and other major governmental buildings are all located in The Hague. Amsterdam began as a fishing village in the thirteenth century. Today, it is a major business and financial center. It is also a major tourist draw, with people coming from all over the world to enjoy its narrow streets and beautiful canals, which are spanned by about 1,300 bridges. They visit notable sites such as the Old Church, the Rijksmuseum, and the Van Gogh Museum.

The nation's second-largest city is Rotterdam (below), home to more than 600,000 people. Rotterdam, today one of the world's largest seaports, developed as a small fishing village after the Rotte River was dammed in the late 1200s. The city quickly grew to become a

major trading center, and today shipping remains the most important part of its economy. Rotterdam suffered heavy bombing in World War II, and the city center was rebuilt according to a new plan. Today, Rotterdam is renowned for its modern architectural landmarks, such as the Market Hall and the Erasmus Bridge. It also features many distinguished museums, including the Museum Boijmans van Beuningen, which features a fantastic collection of European art.

The Hague, the Netherlands' seat of government, is the nation's third-largest city, home to about 510,000 people.

Utrecht, with a population of nearly 330,000, is the Netherlands' fourth-largest city. People have lived on the site of Utrecht for more than two thousand years, and it has long been a religious center in the Netherlands. The Dom Tower, which was built in the 1300s, is its most notable landmark. Utrecht is also an educational center, and Utrecht University is the largest university in the nation.

CHAPTER 3

The Natural World

THE AREA THAT IS NOW THE NETHERLANDS WAS ONCE home to a variety of large creatures, such as the European wild horse, that went extinct long ago. Today, few large natural areas remain in the Netherlands. Almost 65 percent of the country is used for farming, and cities and towns spread across other lands. This makes it a challenging landscape for large wildlife.

Opposite: **Male red deer have large antlers. The deer grow the antlers quickly and then shed them at the end of winter each year.**

Wild Things

Elk survive in or near forested parts of the country. The Hoge Veluwe National Park near Arnhem, in the central part of the country, is home to red deer and wild boar.

Most Netherland dwarf
rabbits are pets. These
rabbits were first bred by
crossing domestic rabbits
with small wild rabbits.

Many smaller animals, including rodents, bats, birds, and reptiles still thrive in the Netherlands. One of the country's most interesting animals is the Netherland dwarf rabbit. This tiny creature weighs less than 2 pounds (1 kilogram) and grows to a mere 3 inches (8 cm) long. These docile animals make great pets.

The Netherlands is home to a wide variety of sea creatures. The long-finned pilot whale can often be seen cavorting off-shore in the North Sea. Although called a whale, it is actually a porpoise. Pilot whales have strong family bonds. When one whale becomes stranded on the beach, the rest of its pod, or family group, often follow and become stranded as well.

Fishing is popular in the Netherlands. Anglers seek white-fish, perch, and pike in the canals and rivers, along with less familiar species such as zander, asp, and ide. Trout and eels thrive in saltwater lakes.

Long-finned pilot whales are extremely social and often live in groups of dozens of creatures.

The merlin, a small falcon common in the Netherlands, often preys on smaller birds.

Among the many types of birds found in the Netherlands are merlins, wood larks, wrens, barn swallows, jackdaws, and swans. The country's vast system of waterways is home to red-crested pochards, black-headed gulls, and cormorants, all feeding in and around the canals and backwaters. Black-tailed godwits wade through the shallow water, snatching up insects and other prey with their long beaks. Many species of geese thrive in the Netherlands, including the pink-footed, the white-fronted, the snow, the bar-headed, the barnacle, the brent, the red-breasted, and the Egyptian goose.

Many reptiles also make the Netherlands their home. Grass snakes, pool frogs, and sand lizards are found hiding in the reeds. Amphibians such as yellow-bellied toads move around in ponds and the nearby mud.

Trees and Flowers

About 11 percent of the land in the Netherlands is forested. Elsewhere in the Netherlands are stands of trees including birch, sweet cherry, silver and giant fir, China jute, Scots pine, maples, box elders, and horse chestnuts. Sycamores and alders shade city streets, with rosebushes and fruit trees dotting expansive parks. The tallest trees in the Netherlands are

Planting a Forest

The Netherlands has planted thick stands of evergreens over about 7 percent of the countryside to prevent erosion. The Amsterdam Forest was created on a polder 13 feet (4 m) below sea level. The planting of the forest began in 1934. More than twenty thousand workers planted 150 varieties of trees to make this forest. The project provided much-needed jobs during the Great Depression, a time when the economy around the world was in a severe slump. In 1970, the last trees in the forest were planted, and the forest is now mature. The forest is home to more than two hundred species of birds. Its branches shade 125 miles (200 km) of hiking trails and 32 miles (50 km) of bicycle paths. Lovers of the outdoors can also row canoes and ride horses in this area in the summer, and ski there in the winter.

several Douglas firs at the grounds of Het Loo Palace in the central part of the country. The loftiest of these firs towers 163 feet (50 m) high.

Amsterdam is proud to be called the City of Trees. More than seventy-five thousand elms provide comforting shade along the backstreets and canals. The people of Amsterdam greatly value their trees. Damaging trees has been a crime since 1454, and residents need a permit to cut one down.

Huge areas of the Het Loo Palace grounds are covered in thick forest.

Famous for Flowers

Brightly colored flowers are everywhere in the Netherlands. Amsterdam's Flower Market is among the most colorful places, with flowers sold from floating barges on the canals. The Amsterdam Tulip Museum pays homage to the tulip, the most famous of all Dutch flowers, and is a great place to learn of the bloom's history. The Dutch tulip season officially kicks off every year in mid-January with National Tulip Day, when thousands of Amsterdam residents pick their own tulips from a special garden. Amsterdam's Tulip Days are held in early May, showcasing fifteen expansive gardens. To see other flowers, visitors flock to the Hortus Botanicus, a botanical garden that features six thousand plant species. Every year at the Keukenhof, the world's second-largest flower garden, seven million flowers bloom, splashing color across dozens of acres just south of Haarlem in the western part of the country.

CHAPTER 4

Over the Years

IMAGINE IT IS TEN THOUSAND YEARS AGO. IT IS SUMMER in northern Europe, in what is now the Netherlands. A flock of ducks soars overhead as red deer bound across a grassy plain. The North Sea roars in the distance, and a soft blanket of warm fog blankets the marshes and dunes along the coast. A band of hunters and gatherers have set up a camp. They have selected this site because it is next to a shallow stretch of the Eem River. The hunters know that the shallow crossing lies along the shortest route across the low swampy ground to the eastern higher ground where game is plentiful. In the camp, meat is smoking over a small fire, and children are chipping away at bones to make tools. Called to eat, one boy drops his half-finished project. The next morning, after a full night's sleep comfortably wrapped in bundles of furs, the band moves on. The child's lost implement is forgotten.

Opposite: **Dutch archaeologists carefully clean off a Roman ship found near Utrecht. It dates to the second century CE.**

9 Vissers- of ijsklompen
Fishermen's ice clogs

The Wooden Shoe Museum in Zaandam, near Amsterdam, displays fishermen's ice clogs and other historic shoes. Some are more than five hundred years old.

Thousands of years later, an archaeological team from the Dutch National Museum of Antiquities arrives on the scene. The scientists are exploring the campsite remains, discovered near today's city of Amersfoort. Artifacts found here, such as the boy's long-lost tool, will be added to the thousands of items at the museum.

Many Migrations

For many thousands of years, people moved through what is now the Netherlands but did not make permanent settlements there. The flooding and cold prevented anyone from settling down too long in one place. Not until about 4500 to 4000 BCE did people from central Europe migrate into this area and build the first primitive villages. Over the next thousand years, more people arrived and clusters of huts grew into villages. The settlers planted crops, including an early form of wheat.

Around 300 BCE, Celts and Germanic Teutons pushed their way north across Europe through the marshes and low-lands. Reaching the North Sea coast, the Celts edged their way west while the Teutons headed east. One Teutonic tribe, the Frisians, were great cattle breeders. Over the next few hundred years, these people extended their power throughout the area. They eventually forced out most of the Celts, who headed across the North Sea to make new homes on the more remote

The Teutons are believed to have originated in Scandinavia. Over time, they migrated through much of western Europe.

A Friesian Cow

From the rugged, rangy ancient cattle bred by Frisian and Saxon clans in the ancient Low Countries, the modern Friesian cow has become a marvelous munching machine. It is able to sustain itself grazing on both low-lying and upland grassland. This makes it the perfect cow for the Netherlands. Over the centuries, two major varieties were developed: one is white with black patches and the other is white with red patches. Friesians are well known for the quality of their milk and lean meat.

island of Great Britain. In 57 BCE, the Romans, marching up from their strongholds in Gaul, now France, allied themselves with some of the Teutons. The Frisians traded cattle hides and horns to the Romans.

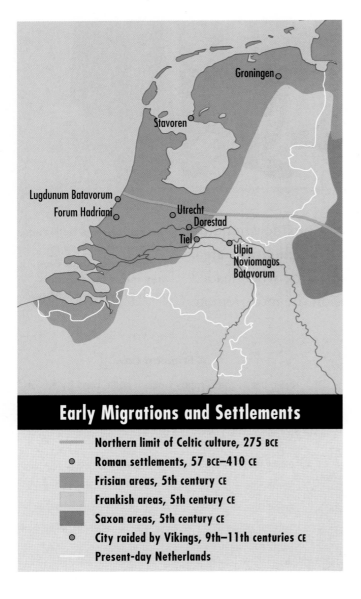

Early Migrations and Settlements

——	Northern limit of Celtic culture, 275 BCE
⊙	Roman settlements, 57 BCE–410 CE
	Frisian areas, 5th century CE
	Frankish areas, 5th century CE
	Saxon areas, 5th century CE
⊙	City raided by Vikings, 9th–11th centuries CE
——	Present-day Netherlands

The Franks were the next people to enter the Low Countries. They stormed out of the East to settle along the Rhine River. Using their military skills, the Franks quickly became the major power along the North Sea. Their Franconian dialect is the root of the contemporary Dutch language.

Rather than resist the Franks, the Frisians moved their herds farther west, settling along the seacoast and nearby islands. Anglo-Irish monks soon arrived to convert the Frisians to Christianity. By 700 CE, the Frisians had become great traders, sailing their merchant vessels as far away as the Baltic Sea.

Their riches attracted the attention of Vikings, who roared out of their Scandinavian strongholds to the north to raid the Frisian settlements. The Vikings' sleek "dragon ships" easily sailed both on the high

seas and up rivers far inland. By the early 1000s, the raids had mostly ended, and many Viking people settled in the Netherlands.

The Frankish emperor Charlemagne united the region for a time, but after he died in 814 his empire collapsed. His kingdom was divided into what would become Germany and France. The Low Countries were divided between the two.

In their sturdy ships, Vikings ranged as far as northern North America and the eastern Mediterranean Sea.

Growing Cities

The first dikes were constructed in the 1100s, expanding the commercial possibilities for the region. Towns grew and a strong merchant class developed. The church, the nobility, and the business community worked together closely to maintain their elite status. They believed that political peace meant commercial peace and prosperity, which in turn led to spiritual peace. Many residents of the Low Countries proved to be skilled businesspeople. While peasants elsewhere in Europe

Under the Hanseatic League, trade flourished in busy ports along the North Sea.

barely scraped by, most of the people in the Low Countries lived in ever-expanding towns. These communities evolved into major crossroads cities.

In the 1100s and 1200s, the Hanseatic League, made up of wealthy cities, came together as an economic powerhouse. The league's power provided protection from pirates, and trading benefits among its partners. *Hanse* was a medieval German word for "guild," or "association."

Burgundians and Habsburgs

Despite stability brought by the league and the demand for increased trade, Europe was in turmoil throughout the thirteenth century. Nation-states battled for power, with every nobleman wanting to expand his influence. The French dukes of Burgundy were among the most aggressive. Philip the Bold and his son John the Fearless used intermarriage, war, and land purchases to extend their influence, especially in the Low Countries. The idea of a strong central government became popular, especially for the business classes that needed peace and stability to achieve commercial

Although never actually king, Philip the Bold was for many years the most powerful man in France.

success. Many communities formed local assemblies consisting of landowners, nobles, merchants, and church officials to work out rules of law. By the mid-1400s, Philip III, known as Philip the Good, controlled wide swaths of territory in the region. Deputies from several assemblies came together to discuss common concerns. These meetings grew into the States General, which evolved into the contemporary Dutch parliament.

Philip III reigned for forty-eight years.

An early meeting of the
council that became the
Dutch parliament

Despite these efforts to discuss issues calmly instead of fighting, there was still a great deal of behind-the-scenes political maneuvering by the European upper classes. Mary of Burgundy, Philip's granddaughter, married Archduke Maximilian of the House of Habsburg, a royal dynasty based in Germany and Austria, in 1477. This linked the Low Countries to the Habsburgs' ever-expanding influence. By the 1500s, the Habsburg heir Charles V reigned over much of Europe, including Germany, Spain, Italy, and the Low Countries. Because Charles's realm was so vast, he appointed local political leaders to keep an eye on the provinces of what are now the Netherlands and Belgium.

The Great Thinker

Desiderius Erasmus (1466-1536) was one of the most influential scholars in Europe during the Renaissance era. He was a Catholic priest and noted linguist from Rotterdam who traveled widely and criticized abuses within the church. He had a devoted following who appreciated liberty more than religious orthodoxy, making him a perfect theologian for the individualistic Dutch. Erasmus's most famous book was *The Praise of Folly*, a mocking look at the beliefs and abuses of the Roman Catholic Church. No other Renaissance figure went as far in making fun of powerful institutions.

Religious Change

The population of the Low Countries was fiercely independent and delighted in learning what was happening in the wider world around them. Through their scholarly writings, thoughtful theologians such as Blessed John of Ruysbroeck (1293–1381) and philosophers like Geert Groote of Deventer (1340–1384) encouraged openness. They also advocated living simply, along with being pious and humble.

At this time, the only form of Christianity in western Europe was Roman Catholicism. As time went on, Catholic bishops and cardinals flaunted their wealth. Church officials sometimes acted more like princes or politicians than religious leaders. Ordinary worshippers in the pews grumbled about the church properties that had grown into magnificent estates. Many people were objecting to some church practices, such as the selling of what were known as indulgences, which would completely forgive sins.

Some church leaders, such as John Brugman, rallied against what they saw as outrageous conduct of other church leaders. In the 1500s, Brugman was renowned for his preaching. To this day, in the Netherlands the saying "to speak like Brugman" is praise for speaking eloquently. The church didn't appreciate Brugman's opinions. They considered reformers such as Brugman to be heretics, people who opposed official doctrine. Yet Brugman and others continued to speak their minds. They wanted to reform the Catholic Church, and their efforts grew into a full-fledged religious rebellion called the Protestant Reformation.

Some Protestants in the 1500s believed that the statues and other art in Catholic churches were a form of idol worship. In 1566, they destroyed the art in many churches in the Netherlands.

John Calvin, a French religious thinker, was a central figure in the development of Protestantism in the 1500s.

Early in the reign of Charles V, the Low Countries generally stayed out of this growing religious furor. But when devotees of Martin Luther, a German priest who was leading the criticism of the Roman Catholic Church, started preaching in his kingdom, Charles set out to destroy the reform movement. He began persecuting the dissidents. The aging Charles retired in 1555, but his legacy of terror was carried on by his son Philip II of Spain. Philip increased religious and political persecution in the Low Countries, raised taxes, and placed Spanish troops in Dutch towns. Thousands fled their country for safety, flocking anywhere they could to escape Philip's aggressive control.

Despite this, ideas advanced by reformers such as John Calvin, a pastor and theologian, slowly took root, mostly in the northern Low Countries. Calvin believed that people were saved only by the grace of God and that nothing else mattered.

Toward Independence

The reform movement provided an excuse for the nobility to stir up the population. The nobility wanted the people of the Low Countries to rise up against Catholic Spain. William I of Orange and other Dutch nobles revolted in 1568. This was the beginning of the Eighty Years' War, a long war for Dutch independence. As more Spanish soldiers marched into the Low Countries, an increasing number of Dutch people supported the rebellion. William and his allies plundered Spanish ships. By 1572, they had captured the provinces of Zeeland and Holland, along the southern coast.

Spanish soldiers loot a village in the Low Countries during the Eighty Years' War.

Despite their religious differences, Protestants and Catholics in the Netherlands joined forces to fight the Spanish occupiers. Representatives of the provinces came together and signed the Pacification of Ghent on November 8, 1576, which firmly established freedom of religion in the Netherlands. Dissenters of all kinds from around Europe subsequently flocked to the Netherlands to escape persecution. In the following year, the parliament of the Netherlands signed the first Union of Brussels, linking the provinces politically. The provinces voted to reject the Spanish governor unless

Dutch ships defeated Spanish forces during the Battle of Gibraltar in 1607. It was the first major naval victory for the Netherlands during the Eighty Years' War.

Saving the Netherlands

William I of Orange was born in 1533 and inherited the princedom of Orange, in France. From age twelve, he was educated in the court of Charles V. William had been raised a Catholic, but later became a Lutheran, and then a Calvinist.

Even when he was still Catholic himself, William did not believe it was acceptable for King Philip II to persecute people for holding religious views that were not Catholic. William ended up leading the Dutch revolt against Spain and helped found the Dutch Republic. In 1580, Philip II placed a bounty on his head, but William was not frightened. He declared that his resistance was justified because the king was a tyrant. In 1584, Philip got his revenge when William was shot to death by an assassin. According to legend, William's final words were, "My God, have pity on my soul; my God, have pity on this poor people." For his efforts in bringing the Low Countries together, William is considered the founder of the Dutch Republic.

Philip called back his troops and agreed to Dutch demands for religious freedom. He grudgingly accepted their terms. Finally, there was peace, however tenuous.

Religious disputes remained. The three southernmost provinces, which eventually became Belgium, remained Catholic. They declared their loyalty to the Spanish king in 1579. That same year, the seven northern provinces of Friesland, Overijssel, Utrecht, Zeeland, Gelderland, Groningen, and Holland formed a union of their own. They signed the Union of Utrecht in 1579, announcing that they were to be called the

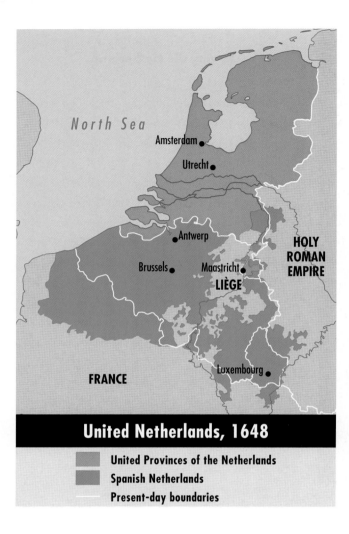

United Netherlands, 1648

- United Provinces of the Netherlands
- Spanish Netherlands
- Present-day boundaries

United Provinces of the Netherlands. Although this new "nation" did not have a ruler, William I was named its civilian administrator. This governmental model marked another important step toward today's Dutch political system.

Spain refused to recognize the United Provinces. A resulting war dragged on from 1579 to 1609, draining money on all sides.

Growing Trade

In 1648, the Spanish king signed the Peace of Westphalia. Under this agreement, the Spanish king finally recognized the Netherlands as a free and independent country. Spain also surrendered its colonies in the Caribbean to the Dutch, who capitalized on these opportunities to create a Golden Age of Commerce.

The Dutch had a thriving trade economy for centuries. Goods from Europe's interior flowed out from Dutch ports to other parts of the world, while wares from around the world entered Dutch harbors and moved inland via canals or carts. With its coastal location in western Europe, the Netherlands' prime location provided the impetus for commercial growth. Amsterdam became Europe's business capital.

Taking advantage of the Netherlands' excellent location, in 1602 wealthy merchants founded the Dutch East India Company (Verenigde Oost-Indische Compagnie, or VOC, in Dutch). The company even had the power to make treaties with foreign rulers. The parliament of the Netherlands also granted VOC a twenty-one-year monopoly for trade activities in Asia. This helped the Netherlands become the world's major commercial hub of that era.

By the mid-1600s, the Netherlands had economic footholds in Southeast Asia, the Caribbean, South America, and the southern tip of Africa. They established colonies in what are now Indonesia, Suriname, and South Africa.

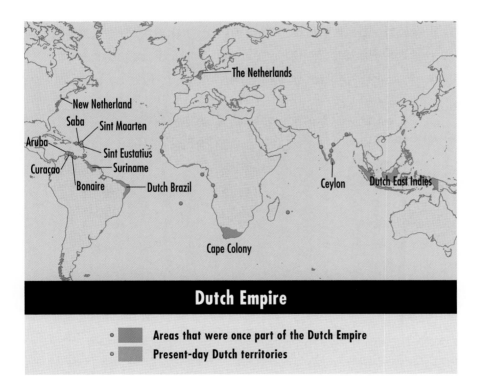

Dutch Empire

Areas that were once part of the Dutch Empire

Present-day Dutch territories

Around the World

Although travel was slow, Dutch traders went all around the world. Sailors wrote home about their adventures, the hardships, and the excitement of dealing with different cultures.

Seaports of that era were dirty, loud, bustling, dangerous, and exciting. People from all corners of the world worked on the ships and at the docks and warehouses of Rotterdam and Amsterdam. It was a risky business. Ships might sink in a storm or be captured by pirates. Sailors could easily lose their lives and merchants could lose their fortunes.

Power Struggles

All this did not end disagreements between the provinces, political factions, and religious organizations. A group of merchants known as Republicans worried that the House of Orange wanted to return a king to power. Led by Republican

Governor of New Netherland

Born in the Netherlands in 1592, Peter Stuyvesant served in the Dutch army in the Caribbean. He was appointed governor of the island colony of Curaçao and lost his right leg in a battle with the Portuguese. For his service, he became the Dutch director-general of the colony of New Netherland in North America from 1647 until it was handed over to the English in 1664. The colony was then renamed New York. The English allowed Stuyvesant to stay on his estate on Manhattan Island until his death in 1672.

Johan De Witt, the Orange contingent was defeated. Yet a mob murdered De Witt when Dutch armies under his command were defeated by the French and English in 1672, which the Dutch of that day called the "year of disaster." The States General then made William III, prince of Orange, a *stadtholder*, or governor. William pushed back the French and recaptured Dutch lands that had been lost.

William's wife, Mary, was also heir to the English throne, so she and her husband became joint rulers of England in 1689. The royal couple kept the French at bay in the following years, but William died without an heir in 1702. Because the Netherlands did not have a strong leader, it did not have much of a voice in the ensuing peace talks. In the eighteenth century, the Dutch lost much of their economic and political power. The Netherlands became a target when Napoleon Bonaparte became ruler of the French in the early 1800s. In 1806, Napoleon claimed the Netherlands as part of his kingdom and installed his brother Louis as king and used the term *Holland* to refer to the entire Netherlands. Louis, however, did not lead as Napoleon had expected. He was sympathetic to the Dutch. He refused to force Dutch soldiers to enlist in the French army and called himself Lodewijk, using

French leader Napoleon Bonaparte dominated Europe in the early 1800s.

the Dutch spelling of his name. Napoleon removed his brother from the throne in 1810. With that, the Netherlands disappeared into the French Empire.

Defeats on the European battlefield weakened Napoleon. Dutch politicians felt it was time to demand freedom again, so they established a constitutional monarchy. William V's son became King William I of the Netherlands.

In 1815, after the fall of Napoleon, Belgium and Luxembourg were added to the new kingdom. But the Belgians rebelled against Dutch rule in 1830. Although reluctant, William agreed to the division of his kingdom and even allowed Belgium to take control of parts of Luxembourg. The remaining portion became the Duchy of Luxembourg, with William its grand duke.

Changing Times

In the decades that followed, Dutch kings worked hard to bolster their country's economy. They constructed additional canals and improved dikes. William II, who reigned for much of the 1840s, ordered that a new constitution be written. The constitution of 1848 gave greater power to the parliament, established the direct election of representatives, and ensured some basic rights, such as the freedom of assembly.

As the economy of the Netherlands grew in the 1800s, grand hotels were built in cities such as The Hague.

William III, who ascended the throne in 1849, disliked the new constitution because he thought it enacted too great a limitation on royal power. During his reign, he sometimes dismissed Parliament, trying to gather more power for himself.

Wilhelmina reigned longer than any other Dutch monarch. She was on the throne for fifty-eight years.

King William III died in 1890 and was succeeded by his daughter, ten-year-old Wilhelmina. The Netherlands allowed women to become monarchs, but Luxembourg did not. As a result, the grand duchy went its own way, finally ending its alliance with the Netherlands. For the initial years of her reign, Wilhelmina's mother acted as regent, a person appointed to administer a country whenever the monarch is a child or is too sick to rule.

The Dutch loved Wilhelmina as their queen. They respected her wisdom, creativity, and good cheer. Through her skillful diplomacy, Wilhelmina kept the Netherlands neutral during World War I and encouraged political and economic reforms after the war. She supported extended voting rights and improving conditions for workers.

Workers at a diamond-cutting factory in Amsterdam in 1911. The diamond industry had been important in Amsterdam since the 1500s.

German troops drive through Amsterdam in 1940.

Depression and War

In the 1930s, worldwide economic downturn shook the Netherlands, and the world. The Great Depression dealt a terrible blow to the country. Many people lost their jobs, their savings, and their homes as banks shut down and businesses collapsed.

People all over the world were desperate and suffering. In this difficult time, Adolf Hitler and his Nazi Party came to power in Germany. Hitler was strongly nationalistic, and he wanted to expand Germany's borders. In 1939, Germany invaded Poland. The United Kingdom, France, and other nations stepped in to help defend Poland by declaring war on Germany. World War II had begun.

The Netherlands again hoped to remain neutral, but Hitler's troops stormed into the country on May 10, 1940, and Dutch resistance collapsed in five days. The great city of Rotterdam was bombed into ruins, with thousands of civilian casualties. Queen Wilhelmina barely escaped the devastation, fleeing to Great Britain.

Even after Germany gained control of the Netherlands, many Dutch people continued to struggle against their occupiers. Dutch resistance fighters cut telephone wires and killed German military personnel.

As German forces invaded the Netherlands in May 1940, they bombed Rotterdam. In a single day, almost all of the city's historic center was destroyed.

Remembering Anne

Adolf Hitler and the Nazi Party were deeply anti-Semitic, meaning they held a deep hatred toward Jewish people. It became their policy to try to rid Europe of Jews. In carrying out this policy, the Nazis killed six million European Jews. Many of them died in death camps.

Almost every Jewish person in the Netherlands was sent to death camps, despite efforts by many Dutch people to hide their friends, neighbors, and sometimes strangers. Anne Frank was a young Jewish girl in Amsterdam who hid from the Nazis. A bookcase (right) concealed a door that led to the attic where she hid. Anne wrote about her experiences, and some of her words are as uplifting today as they were when she wrote them:

"I looked out of the open window, over a large area of Amsterdam, over all the roofs and on to the horizon, which was such a pale blue that it was hard to see the dividing line. As long as this exists, I thought, and I may live to see it, this sunshine, these cloudless skies, while this lasts I cannot be unhappy."

Anne did not survive the war. German police discovered Anne and her family in 1944, and she died in a concentration camp in Germany the following year. Her father, however, survived, and when he returned to the house where his family had hidden, he found that Anne's diary had been saved. Anne Frank's *The Diary of a Young Girl* was first published in 1947 and has since been published in sixty languages. Anne's former home is now a museum.

After the War

The Allies defeated Germany in 1945. Although the Netherlands was free from German control, the country was in ruins. The Dutch immediately set about to repair the damage. Cities were rebuilt, and the country became increasingly industrialized. The Netherlands produced steel, chemicals, and electronic goods.

The years after World War II saw increasing pressure on European nations to end their colonial rule of people around the world. The Netherlands still held colonies in Southeast Asia, South America, and the Caribbean. In 1949, the Dutch colonies in Southeast Asia demanded independence. After

German soldiers leave the Netherlands following the German surrender in May 1945.

Sukarno, the first Indonesian president, addresses a huge crowd in the city of Jakarta during the Indonesian struggle for independence from the Netherlands.

strongly objecting at first, the Netherlands eventually gave in to international pressure and released its centuries-old grip on Sumatra, Java, Borneo, and Sulawesi. These islands and others united to form the single country of Indonesia.

In 1975, the Netherlands granted independence to its South American colony of Suriname. In the years that followed, the Caribbean islands held by the Netherlands became gradually more independent.

Recent Times

When Suriname became independent, many people who lived there feared that a civil war would break out between rival factions. As a result, more than 130,000 Surinamese people moved to the Netherlands. Although Suriname did not erupt into war, the refugees stayed in Europe. Many people from Indonesia, Turkey, and Morocco also settled in the Netherlands.

Most Dutch people welcomed the immigrants. But as the immigrant population grew, some Dutch people worried that the newcomers were not accepting Dutch culture. Recent immigrants must now take a test showing that they understand the Dutch language and society.

Despite these tensions, the Netherlands retains its reputation for openness and tolerance. For example, in 2001, it became the first nation in the world to legalize same-sex marriage.

Moving into the future, the Netherlands will continue to face many difficult problems, from rising sea levels to rising health care costs. The Dutch will likely tackle these problems head-on, as they always have.

Three couples cut their wedding cake after taking their marriage vows at the Amsterdam city hall on April 1, 2001, the first day that same-sex marriage was allowed in the Netherlands.

CHAPTER 5

The Government at Work

THE KINGDOM OF THE NETHERLANDS IS GOVERNED according to a constitution that dates to 1814. The constitution lays out the form of the government and the basic rights of the people. Because of changing circumstances, the document has been regularly updated. For example, civil rights protections have been added, and the death penalty has been abolished. Both houses of the States General must approve any changes to the document. The constitution divides the government into three branches: executive, legislative, and judicial.

Executive Branch

According to the constitution, the government of the Netherlands is a constitutional monarchy. In a monarchy, the head of state is a king or queen whose power is limited by a constitution. In the Netherlands, the monarch is mostly a figurehead. The nation is a democracy where the real governing power lies with elected leaders.

In the Netherlands, the duties of the monarch are mostly ceremonial. However, the current king, Willem-Alexander, keeps a close eye on what is happening politically, socially, and culturally in the country. He has weekly meetings with the prime minister and chats regularly with other ministers, signs all new Acts of Parliament and royal decrees, and approves international treaties.

The monarch also presides over the Council of State, which can have up to ten members. The heir to the throne becomes a member of the council at age eighteen, so he or she can begin learning the workings of the government. The Council of State provides the government and Parliament with independent advice on legislation and governance and doubles as the country's highest administrative court. Following intense discussions within the council, the king or queen can issue a royal decree, which is countersigned by a cabinet minister. The council's vice president would become acting head of state if there were no monarch to assume the throne. The council was established in 1531, making it one of the oldest active governmental bodies in the world.

The prime minister is the head of government, in charge of coordinating government policy and running the daily workings of the country. Most often, the prime minister is leader of the party with the most seats in the House of Representatives, one of the two branches of Parliament. He or she chooses members of a cabinet, whose duty is to decide how the government should function by overseeing the various governmental departments. Second in charge after the prime minister is the

A Look at The Hague

According to the constitution, Amsterdam is the capital of the Netherlands. But unlike most national capitals, it is not the seat of government. Instead, the parliament, the Supreme Court, and other major government buildings are in The Hague. The city has grown quickly in the last century, and today is home to about 510,000 people. Government and business are the major industries in The Hague.

The Hague is located on the site of a castle built in 1248. The buildings surrounding this castle, where nobility lived, are known as the Binnenhof (Inner Court, below). Among the city's other monuments are the Noordeinde Palace, which dates to the sixteenth century, and the Mauritshuis, which features artworks of great Dutch painters such as Rembrandt and Vermeer.

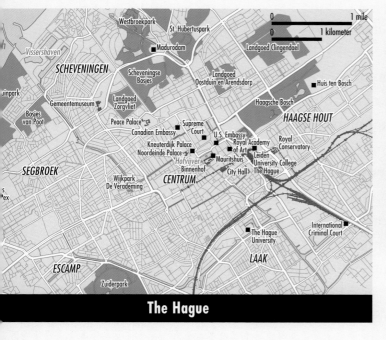

The Hague

To the Throne

When King Willem-Alexander was crowned on April 30, 2013, he became the first man to serve as the monarch of the Netherlands in more than 120 years. He succeeded his mother, Beatrix, who had served as monarch for thirty-three years. In the Netherlands, the firstborn child of the monarch is heir to the throne, whether a boy or a girl.

King Willem-Alexander is married to Queen Máxima, who was born in Argentina and has dual Dutch-Argentine citizenship. She has degrees in economics and has worked in international finance. The couple has three daughters, Catharina-Amalia, Alexia, and Ariane. All three Dutch princesses attend regular public school like any other child in the Netherlands.

minister of finance. Other cabinet ministers manage interior and kingdom relations, foreign affairs, defense, infrastructure and the environment, social affairs and employment, security and justice, economic affairs, and health, welfare, and sport. A secretary-general manages the office's day-to-day operations.

Legislative Branch

The States General, the lawmaking body in the Netherlands, includes two parts. The First Chamber, also called the Senate, has seventy-five members who are elected to four-year terms by the legislatures of the Netherlands' twelve provinces. The Second Chamber, also called the House of Representatives, has 150 members, whom voters elect to four-year terms. Under the Dutch system, each political party receives a share of seats in the Second Chamber based on the number of votes its list of candidates received.

The Netherlands has at least twelve major parties and several minor ones. The largest parties include the People's Party for Freedom and Democracy, Christian Democratic Appeal, and the Labor Party. Because there are so many parties, it is nearly impossible for one party to win a majority of seats in the chamber. As a result, many different parties work together on legislation. These proposed laws are passed along to the First Chamber, which can accept or reject them. The First Chamber cannot, however, propose laws itself.

The members of the House of Representatives belong to about a dozen different political parties.

Workers count votes following an election in The Hague.

Dutch citizens who are eighteen or older can vote in elections. Foreigners who are legal residents of the Netherlands may vote in some local elections. The Dutch take their voting responsibility seriously. In the 2012 parliamentary elections, about 74 percent of eligible voters turned out, casting more than nine million votes.

Judicial Branch

The judicial system in the Netherlands includes eleven district courts, five courts of appeal, and one Supreme Court, as well as lower courts for minor offenses. There are no jury trials in the Netherlands. Single judges preside over minor cases, with several justices making up a tribunal to handle more important cases.

The National Government of the Netherlands

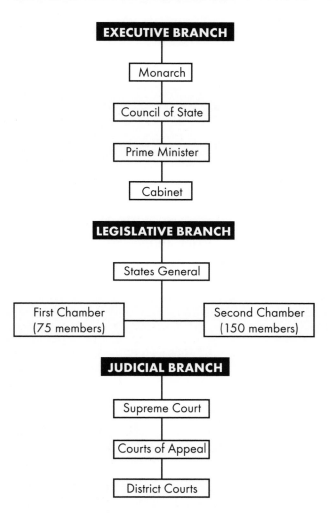

EXECUTIVE BRANCH

Monarch

Council of State

Prime Minister

Cabinet

LEGISLATIVE BRANCH

States General

First Chamber
(75 members)

Second Chamber
(150 members)

JUDICIAL BRANCH

Supreme Court

Courts of Appeal

District Courts

Major cases start at the district court level. The courts of appeal review decisions made in district courts. The Supreme Court is the country's highest judicial body. It ensures that laws are applied fairly. But unlike the U.S. Supreme Court, it does not rule on the constitutionality of laws or treaties. Justices

The National Flag

The flag of the Netherlands consists of three equal horizontal bands of red, white, and blue. The flag stems from a banner used by the House of Orange. Originally, the top band of the flag was orange, but the orange dye was unstable and would often change to red over time, so after 1630, the orange was gradually replaced by a red band. In 1937, the current design was officially adopted as the national flag.

Forty-one justices sit on the Dutch Supreme Court, but usually only five rule on any given case. are appointed by royal decree, with advice by the House of Representatives. Like other judges in the Netherlands, the Supreme Court justices are appointed for life.

Regional and Local Government

The Netherlands has twelve provinces, which are similar to states in the United States and provinces in Canada. The central government appoints a king's commissioner for each province. This person acts as provincial executive and chairs the provincial council. The commissioner also helps select mayors.

In 2014, Dutch king Willem-Alexander (right) swore in Maarten Feteris (left) as the new president of the Supreme Court.

The National Anthem

"Het Wilhelmus" ("The William"), the Dutch national anthem, is one of the oldest national anthems in the world. The melody originated in the 1500s. Although no one is certain who wrote the lyrics, poet and diplomat Marnix van Sint Aldegonde is credited with having written them in the 1570s. The song was officially adopted as the national anthem in 1932.

The song's title refers to William of Orange, the leader of a Dutch revolt against Spain. In the anthem, William talks to the oppressed people of the Netherlands. He affirms his sincerity and determination and explains why he has risen up against the king of Spain.

Dutch lyrics

Wilhelmus van Nassouwe
Ben ik, van Duitsen bloed,
Den vaderland getrouwe
Blijf ik tot in den dood.
Een Prinse van Oranje
Ben ik vrij onverveerd,
Den Koning van Hispanje
Heb ik altijd geëerd.

English translation

William of Nassau, scion
Of a Dutch and ancient line,
I dedicate undying
Faith to this land of mine.
A prince am I undaunted,
Of Orange, ever free,
To the king of Spain I've granted
A lifelong loyalty.

At the local level, Dutch water boards play a key role in environmental management in the Netherlands. They are responsible for managing and maintaining surface water quantity and quality. One of the oldest public authorities in the Netherlands, the twenty-seven boards operate independently from the central government as they fulfill their primary task of safeguarding the country against flooding.

Provinces of the Netherlands

CHAPTER 6

The Dutch at Work

THE NETHERLANDS HAS A THRIVING ECONOMY. FOR centuries, the country has been a center of international trade.

The nation's biggest trading partners include Germany, Belgium, Luxembourg, France, the United Kingdom, the United States, Russia, and China. In 2013, exports from the Netherlands were valued at US$671.8 billion, up 36.4 percent since 2010. The top exports include fuels, machinery, electronic equipment, chemicals, and plastics. Major imports include oil, computers, medicines, and automobiles.

Opposite: **A Dutch worker in the city of Dordrecht, along the coast, puts fabric on a chair. About 16 percent of the country's workforce is employed in industry.**

Working Together

The Netherlands has long been active in European economic cooperation. In 1952, the country joined Belgium, France, Italy, Luxembourg, and what was then West Germany in founding the European Coal and Steel Community (ECSC). At that time, these nations decided it would be better to work together for their common commercial well-being. In 1957, this group established what was then called the European Economic Community, a precursor of today's European Union.

Today, twenty-eight countries are part of the EU. They have a combined population of about 500 million people, making the EU the world's largest single market. Goods and people flow freely across the borders of these countries. The EU has also established policies that all member states follow. These cover areas such as trade and agriculture. Nineteen EU member nations, including the Netherlands, now use a common currency, called the euro.

A Dutch man works on an engine. Repair people work in the service sector of the economy.

The Netherlands is one of nearly twenty nations that use the euro as its currency. Each euro is divided into one hundred cents. The euro currency mark is the symbol €. In 2015, 1 euro equaled US$1.12, and US$1.00 equaled 89 euros.

Banknotes come in 5-, 10-, 20-, 50-, 100-, 200-, and 500-euro denominations, with designs that feature Europe's architectural history. The front sides show windows and gates, while the backs feature bridges. Coins come in values of 1, 2, 5, 10, 20, and 50 cents, as well as 1 and 2 euros.

Agriculture

Agriculture is a major business in the Netherlands. Some six hundred thousand Dutch people work directly or indirectly in the agriculture or food-processing sector. About 75,000 farms supply high-quality produce, meat, and dairy products. The Netherlands produces one-quarter of the vegetables exported from Europe. This amounts to almost 20 percent of the Netherlands' total exports. It is a major producer of tomatoes, potatoes, cucumbers, onions, peppers, apples, and pears. It is the world's top producer of large flowers. The country exports 4.3 billion tulip bulbs each year.

Many Dutch farmers raise animals. There are about 6,500 Dutch pig farms, and many varieties of chickens originated in the Netherlands. The Barnevelders are chickens originally from Barneveld, a community that is now home of the Dutch Poultry Museum. Developed as a breed in the mid-1800s, Barnevelders were known for their production of large brown

Flower Frenzy

The queen of Dutch flowers is the tulip, which is grown in huge numbers by the country's skilled farmers. Tulips were originally cultivated during the Ottoman Empire, centered in Asia, and were imported into the Netherlands in the sixteenth century. As the Dutch economy expanded in the following century, so did the popularity of this colorful flower. In the mid-seventeenth century, tulips became so popular that the demand for them was greater than the supply. In a buying frenzy, some people even sold their own homes to make money with which to snap up the bulbs in the hope of reselling them at a higher price. This time was known as Tulip Mania. Tulips subsequently became so expensive that they were used as currency. Eventually the tulip market crashed, but the Dutch retained their love of this vivid flower.

eggs. Other breeds that were developed in the Netherlands are the Polish, Hamburg, Welsummer, Friesian, and the Dutch Booted Bantams.

Dairy farming is highly developed in the Netherlands, with farmers producing milk, butter, and cheese. Cheese has a long history in the Netherlands. As far back as 1649, the port of Edam was already exporting 1,000,000 pounds (450,000 kg) of cheese a year. Initially, cheese was made in farmers' homes, but today about 800,000 tons (725,000 metric tons) are produced in major processing plants. Much of it is exported. One of the most popular varieties is Gouda, a cheese with creamy flavor, favored by cheese lovers around the world.

Manufacturing and Mining

About one in five Dutch workers is employed in manufacturing. Among the country's major manufacturing industries are food processing and the production of electrical goods, chemicals, metals, petroleum products, and vehicle parts.

The Netherlands has few natural resources, so mining is not a major industry. The country's most valuable resource is natural gas, which lies under the North Sea. The Netherlands also pumps oil from under the North Sea, but not nearly enough to fulfill its need, so it must import large quantities of oil. In addition, the nation produces limestone, zinc, and magnesium. Salt is mined at Overijssel and Groningen.

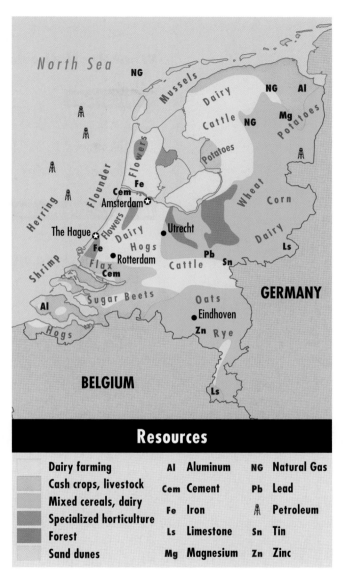

Resources

Dairy farming	Al	Aluminum	NG	Natural Gas
Cash crops, livestock	Cem	Cement	Pb	Lead
Mixed cereals, dairy	Fe	Iron		Petroleum
Specialized horticulture				
Forest	Ls	Limestone	Sn	Tin
Sand dunes	Mg	Magnesium	Zn	Zinc

Fishing

With its long coastline, it is no wonder that fishing is big business in the Netherlands. The Netherlands' North Sea fishing fleet numbers approximately six hundred trawlers and specially outfitted vessels. Headed for the Dutch dinner plates are herring, brill, sole, plaice, haddock, turbot, and shrimp.

What the Netherlands Grows, Makes, and Mines

AGRICULTURE

Potatoes (2013)	6,576,860 metric tons
Tomatoes (2013)	855,000 metric tons
Flowering bulbs and tubers (2012)	212,562 acres

MANUFACTURING (2010, VALUE ADDED)

Food products	US$13,966,000,000
Chemical products	US$13,235,000,000
Machinery	US$12,312,000,000

MINING

Natural gas (2013)	69,516,000,000 cubic meters
Oil (2013)	8,510,000 barrels
Zinc (2012)	257,000 metric tons

Service Industries

The largest part of the Dutch economy is the service sector. People who work in service industries do not grow or make products. Instead, they do something for other people. Bankers, doctors, teachers, waiters, and bus drivers all work in service industries. So does anyone who fixes computers, designs Web sites, or works in an office or store.

Some of the world's largest companies are headquartered in the Netherlands. Royal Dutch Shell is the second-largest petroleum company in the world in terms of revenue. Shell has forty thousand gas stations around the world, many in the United States and Canada, and it operates forty-seven oil refineries.

Another major company, Unilever, produces a huge variety of food and household products. The banking giants ING Group and ABN AMRO are also based in the Netherlands.

Tourism is a major service industry in the Netherlands. In 2014, roughly 14 million foreign visitors arrived in the Netherlands, a 4 percent increase over the previous year. The wide range of museums, festivals, charming cities, and beautiful countryside attract tourists from around the world. The majority of visitors come from nearby European countries,

A guide points out sites to tourists in Amsterdam, the most visited city in the Netherlands.

and a growing number are from Russia and China. In 2014, foreign visitors spent 10.2 billion euros in the Netherlands on everything from hotels to opera tickets to ice cream.

Transportation

It is easy to get to the Netherlands, whether by boat, bus, airplane, or automobile. The Netherlands boasts 86,553 miles (139,294 km) of highways. Railroads crisscross the nation, connecting cities in Amsterdam to the rest of Europe.

A woman shops in a store in the Netherlands. Service industries such as sales make up the largest part of the Dutch economy.

The thirteen major Dutch seaports move more than 500 million metric tons of freight annually. Rotterdam is the largest harbor in Europe. For much of the twentieth century, it was the world's busiest port. The nation's extensive canal and river system connects the interior to the ports on the coast.

Ninety different airlines fly in and out of the Netherlands' twenty-eight major airports. KLM Royal Dutch Airlines is the country's national airline, founded in 1919. Schiphol Airport is the country's largest and busiest, located in the municipality of Haarlemmermeer, just a twenty-minute drive southwest of Amsterdam. Schiphol is the fourth-busiest airport in Europe in terms of passengers. In 2013, more than 52 million passengers traveled through it.

KLM is the world's oldest airline that still operates under its original name.

Communications

The Netherlands has a highly developed communications system. Most people have cell phones, computers, and Internet service.

The Netherlands has six major newspapers. The most widely read is *De Telegraaf*, which is based in Amsterdam but distributed across the nation. About half a million copies of *De Telegraaf* are distributed every day. The *Metro* and *Spits* are free to readers, and they are popular with train and bus commuters. There are more than nine thousand different magazines distributed in the country.

Most people living in the Netherlands have access to at least thirty different TV channels. Viewers enjoy watching the three Dutch public service TV stations, which broadcast educational programs, detective stories, comedies, and more. The Dutch can also tune in to programs from stations in neighboring countries.

People who work at FloraHolland, the world's largest flower auction, rely on computers. In 2014, the Netherlands had the sixth-fastest Internet speed of any country in the world.

CHAPTER 7

People and Language

ALTHOUGH ONLY 16.8 MILLION PEOPLE LIVE IN the Netherlands, it is one of the most crowded nations in the world. An average of 1,048 people live on every square mile of land in the country (405 per sq km). But in fact, for most people it is even more densely populated than that. Half the population lives on just 15 percent of land, in the provinces of North and South Holland.

The Dutch People

The Dutch are among the tallest people in the world. This is due to a combination of their genes, a healthy diet that includes a lot of protein, and a high standard of living. The average Dutch man is 6 feet 1 inch (185 cm) tall, and the average Dutch woman is 5 feet 6½ inches (170 cm) tall.

In recent decades, the population of the Netherlands has become much more diverse. Today, the Dutch population

Opposite: **Crowds fill the streets for a festival in Amsterdam.**

Ethnic Background in the Netherlands (2014 est.)	
Dutch	79%
Turkish	2%
Indonesian	2%
Moroccan	2%
German	2%
Surinamese	2%
Caribbean	1%
Polish	1%
Belgian	1%
Other	8%

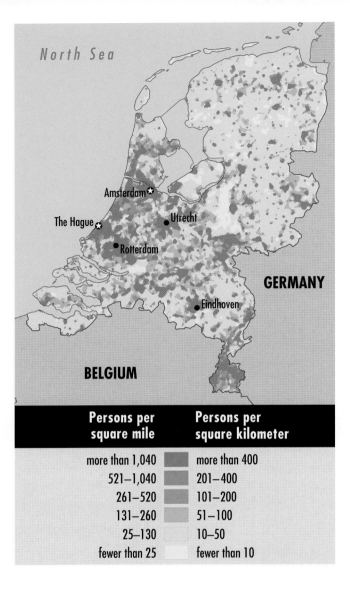

Persons per square mile		Persons per square kilometer
more than 1,040		more than 400
521–1,040		201–400
261–520		101–200
131–260		51–100
25–130		10–50
fewer than 25		fewer than 10

Population of Major Cities (2014 est.)

Amsterdam	810,937
Rotterdam	618,357
The Hague	508,940
Utrecht	328,164
Eindhoven	220,920

includes many people of Indonesian, Surinamese, West African, Turkish, and Moroccan descent. Many of the African and Middle Eastern residents of the Netherlands originally came as guest workers and stayed.

Language

The official language of the Netherlands is Dutch, which is used everywhere. In the province of Friesland, a language called Frisian is also spoken. Frisian has been officially recognized as a minority language of the Netherlands since 1996. Today, about 450,000 people speak it. Both Dutch and Frisian are of Germanic origin. The vocabulary of the Dutch language is similar to German, but the grammar is more closely related to English.

The vast majority of Dutch people can speak more than one language. English, which is a required course in all Dutch high schools, is the most commonly spoken second language. Nearly 90 percent of Dutch people can speak English. Many Dutch people also speak German and French. As more people have immigrated to the Netherlands from around the world, non-European languages have become more commonly spo-

Common Dutch Words and Phrases

Dutch	Pronunciation	English
hallo	hallo	hello
alstublieft	alst oo bleeft	please
dank u wel	dank oo vel	thank you
ja/nee	ya/nay	yes/no
Spreekt u Engels?	Sprect oo engels?	Do you speak English?
Spreekt u Nederlands?	Sprect oo Nederlands?	Do you speak Dutch?
goedemorgen	gudemorgen	good morning
goedenacht	gudenacht	good night

ken in the Netherlands. Many people in Muslim communities are fluent in Turkish or Arabic. Vietnamese, Chinese, Kurdish, Persian, and Malay are also commonly heard.

A sign in Dutch at a park in the Netherlands

Education

The Netherlands has a strong educational system, and 99 percent of people in the country can read and write. Since 1917, schools in the Netherlands have received public funding. Primary and secondary state education is free. Teachers in both public and independent schools are paid the same salary. Parents can choose between public and religious schools. Some schools are Catholic, while others are Protestant, Muslim, or Jewish.

Children in school in The Hague. On average, elementary school classes in the Netherlands have twenty-two students.

School attendance is compulsory for children ages four to eighteen. Some children begin primary school as young as age three and continue with their primary education until they are about twelve years old. They study subjects such as languages, math, social and environmental studies, music, and art. Sports are also encouraged. Children's test scores determine what kind of secondary school they attend. They might get sent to a general, a preuniversity, or a vocational secondary school. Most students graduate at age eighteen.

More than four hundred thousand students are enrolled at dozens of universities in the Netherlands. These include some of the oldest universities in Europe, such as Leiden University, founded in 1575, and the University of Groningen, which was founded in 1614.

Freshmen gather at Utrecht University for orientation in the days before classes start. One of the oldest universities in the Netherlands, it was founded in 1636.

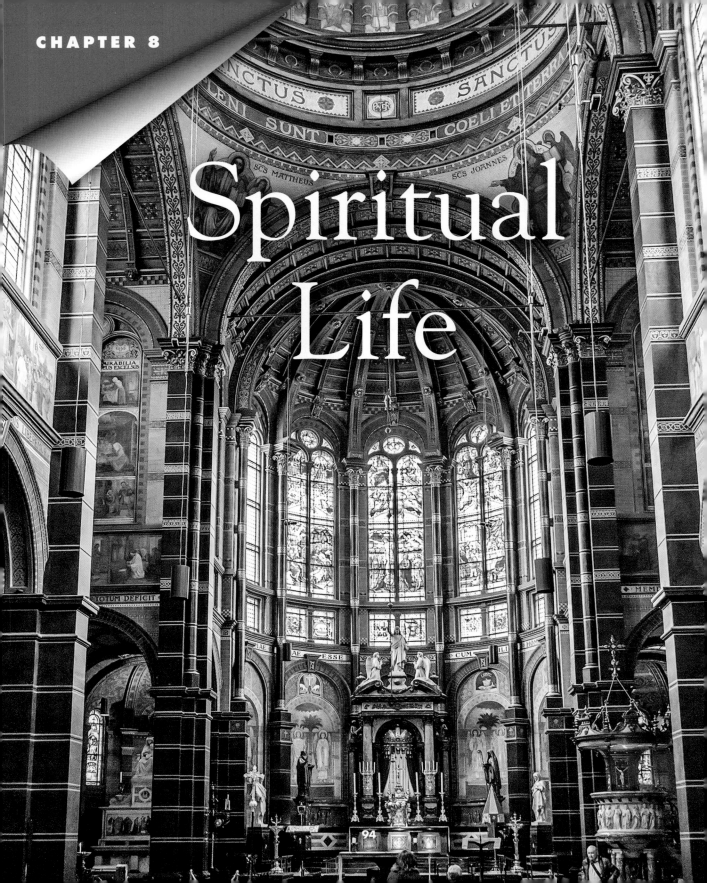

CHAPTER 8

Spiritual Life

THE NETHERLANDS DOES NOT HAVE AN OFFICIAL religion. Throughout history, people of all faiths could freely practice their beliefs. In the 1950s, 80 percent of the Dutch people belonged to a church. But since the 1960s, the Netherlands has seen a sharp decrease in church attendance. Today, almost half the Dutch population professes no religion.

The Arrival of Christianity

Ancestors of today's Dutch were pagans who believed in spirits found in nature. At the start of the sixth century, Christian missionaries from Ireland arrived in what is now the Netherlands. The pagan people were initially suspicious of these Irish monks who preached of one god. However, the local nobility believed that they could increase their power by converting. In 496, Frankish King Clovis I became a Christian and his subjects felt it was wise to join him.

Opposite: **The Basilica of Saint Nicholas is the largest Catholic Church in Amsterdam.**

Willibrord preaches to
the Frisians. He became
the first bishop of
Utrecht in 695.

The Frisians took longer to convert. They retained their traditional beliefs for several more generations. In the late 600s, a missionary named Willibrord came to the Netherlands from Great Britain, and he had more success. His ancestors

Priests lead a Mass in Hengelo, in the eastern Netherlands.

had originated from the same coastal area as the Frisians, and he understood their customs and temperament. Frankish emperor Charlemagne eventually conquered all the remaining pagan groups. They were given two options: Convert or die.

Christianity Today

About 28 percent of Dutch people belong to the Roman Catholic Church. Roman Catholics live primarily in the Netherlands' southern provinces. Catholicism has been declining in the Netherlands for decades. As recently as the 1970s, 40 percent of Dutch people were Catholic. Not only has the number of Catholics dropped, but the number of people who actively participate in church services has also dropped. It is estimated that only about 1 percent of Dutch people attend Mass on any particular Sunday.

Religion in the Netherlands (2009)	
Roman Catholic	28%
Protestant	19%
Muslim	5%
Other	6%
None	42%

Religious Holidays

Good Friday	March or April
Easter Sunday	March or April
Easter Monday	March or April
Passover	March or April
Ascension Day	May or June
Whitsuntide	May or June
Saint Nicholas Day	December 6
Christmas	December 25 and 26

A Dutch Reformed church in the Netherlands. The buildings of the Dutch Reformed Church are very simple.

Roughly 19 percent of the Dutch population is Protestant. Protestants live primarily in the northern part of the country. The Dutch Reformed Church is the largest denomination.

Remembering Jewish History

Established in 1930, the Jewish Historical Museum in Amsterdam has a wide range of permanent and traveling exhibits. Displays have included *The Unknown History of Jews in the Dutch East Indies* and an extensive exhibition on the Jewish communities in Curaçao and Suriname. The museum displays art, ceremonial items, and historical objects. Its research center has more than forty-three thousand books, documents, and audio and video materials for scholarly use.

Founded in the sixteenth century, the church has kept powerful ties with the Dutch elite. All the country's monarchs have belonged to this church. The nation, however, has no official church.

A man lights candles in the Portuguese Synagogue in Amsterdam. When it was completed in 1675, it was one of the largest synagogues in the world.

Judaism

Jewish people have been in the Netherlands for more than four hundred years. Many fled oppression elsewhere in Europe and found a haven in the Netherlands. Among them were Portuguese Jews who established Ets Haim Library in 1616 in Amsterdam. Their descendants include Benedict de Spinoza (1632–1677), one of the greatest philosophers in European history.

About thirty thousand Jews live in the Netherlands today, but that number was once much higher. During World War II, more than one hundred thousand Jews were rounded up by the Nazis and sent to concentration camps and killed. That was about 75 percent of the nation's Jewish population.

The Great Philosopher

Benedict de Spinoza was born in Amsterdam in 1632 to Jewish parents who had moved to the Netherlands from Portugal. As a boy, Spinoza studied Jewish thought, but he eventually became skeptical of some religious ideas. He began to study the works of other philosophers and developed his own ideas. Although Spinoza believed in God, he considered God to be impersonal and distant. He argued instead for rationalism, the idea that knowledge is based on reason and evidence rather than religion and emotion. His writings, such as *Ethics*, proved to be hugely influential. They were central to the ideas of the Enlightenment, a philosophy that dominated Europe in the 1700s and emphasized understanding the world through reason.

A man reads the Qur'an, the holy book of Islam, at a mosque in Amsterdam.

Islam

Since the 1960s, many Muslim immigrants have come to the Netherlands. By 2014, there were almost one million Muslims living in Dutch cities. Many schools have opened to serve the Muslim population. There are thirty-seven Islamic primary schools and one secondary school in Rotterdam alone, plus the privately funded Islamic University of Rotterdam and the Islamic University of Europe in Schiedam.

Muslims are making their presence known in government as cabinet ministers and elected officials. Among the most influential politicians is Ahmed Aboutaleb, who became mayor of Rotterdam in 2009.

CHAPTER 9

Creating and Playing

THE NETHERLANDS HAS PRODUCED SOME OF THE greatest painters the world has ever known. The sixteenth and seventeenth centuries were particularly lively. Hieronymus Bosch (1450–1516) showed the folly of mankind with his triptych *The Garden of Earthly Delights*. Hendrick Avercamp (1585–1634), Johannes Vermeer (1632–1675), and Jan Havicksz Steen (1626–1679) made paintings that depicted everyday life in the Netherlands that are delightful in their reality. They show street scenes, Dutch people eating, working, and playing, and interacting with their animals.

Opposite: **A group of musicians plays on the street in Amsterdam.**

Art

Many people consider the greatest Dutch painter of this era to be Rembrandt van Rijn (1606–1669). His innovative use of light creates vibrancy in each of his canvases, such as *The Night Watch*, which depicts a group of patrolling soldiers. He is also known for his intimate portraits.

Later, Vincent van Gogh (1853–1890) used swift powerful strokes with his brush or palette knife to create masterpieces that reveal deep emotion. Van Gogh produced more than two thousand paintings in just over ten years. He created most of his best-known works, including *The Starry Night* and *Sunflowers*, in the two years before his death. Many of his paintings are displayed in the Van Gogh Museum in Amsterdam and the Kröller-Müller Museum in Otterlo.

Abstract art also has a strong history in the Netherlands. Piet Mondrian, for example, created paintings based on grids. In these works he used only black lines and blocks of red, yellow, and blue.

Other important Dutch artists include book illustrator Anton Pieck, sculptor Theo Jansen, photographer Levi van Veluw, graphic designer Robert Overweg, and architect Rem Koolhaas.

Literature

The romantic novel was a popular literary form for early Dutch authors—both male and female. Elizabeth Bekker Wolff (1738–1804) and Agatha Deken (1741–1804) composed their popular *The History of Miss Sara Burgerhart* in 1782. The story tells the tale of a young woman who runs away from an

Strandbeest, a sculpture by Theo Jansen, is made of plastic tubes and bottles and walks using the power of the wind.

abusive aunt. Eduard Douwes Dekker (1820–1887) wrote the best-selling satire *Max Havelaar* in 1860, decrying the oppressive Dutch rule in the East Indies. Novelist and short story writer Arthur van Schendel (1874–1946) was born in the East Indies and wrote romantic stories that vividly brought to life very specific settings. Marga Minco's *Bitter Herbs*, published

Marga Minco was born into a Jewish family. She spent World War II in hiding and later recounted the experience in her book *Bitter Herbs*.

in 1957, narrates the tale of a young girl during World War II. Novelist and Dutch language professor Cynthia Henri McLeod is the daughter of Johan Ferrier, the first president of Suriname. Her first book, *The Cost of Sugar*, released in 1987, relates the hard life of slaves on the island's sugar plantations in the eighteenth century.

Arnon Grunberg, who was born in 1971, is one of the Netherlands' most celebrated authors and journalists. After visiting Dutch troops in war-torn Afghanistan, he collected his journalistic reports in the gripping book *Chambermaids and Soldiers* in 2009.

Poetry is also thriving in the Netherlands. Readings are popular in bookstores such as Amsterdam's Perdu, and verses are shared over the Internet. Poetry festivals are held in The Hague, Groningen, and Biddinghuizen. A National Day of Poetry is held annually in January and a Week of Poetry is designated each April. Among the best-known contemporary

A thirteenth-century church in Maastricht now houses a bookstore. In 2013, Dutch people bought thirty-nine million books.

poets are Leonard Nolens, Alfred Schaffer, Pieter Boskma, Erwin Mortier, and Wouter Godijn. Born in 1974, Tsead Bruinja is a noted Frisian poet. He often recites in public, backed by hip-hop musicians.

Gerbrand Adriaenszoon Bredero (1585–1618), Govert Bidloo (1649–1713), and the prolific Joost van den Vondel (1587–1679), honored for his works promoting religious tolerance, are among the earliest playwrights in the Dutch theater world. They have been followed by dozens of other creative writers. Gerrit Komrij (1944–2012) was born in Winterswijk and became a well-known literary critic, translator, poet, and playwright.

Music

The Dutch have also made their mark in music. The Netherlands has a strong tradition of classical music. The Royal Concertgebouw Orchestra has been considered among the world's best since its founding in 1888. Traveling widely, the symphony reaches around 250,000 concertgoers a year. The Netherlands Radio Philharmonic Orchestra is another award-winning Dutch musical institution, founded in 1945. The Netherlands Chamber Orchestra and Netherlands Bach Society both attract a fervent following.

The Royal Concertgebouw Orchestra rehearses in Amsterdam.

People in the Netherlands also enjoy jazz and many varieties of rock and roll. The Tielman Brothers and the Blue Diamonds were pioneers on the Dutch rock scene in the late 1950s. In the 1960s, concertgoers jumped up from their seats whenever Golden Earring, Shocking Blue, Epica, and Focus took the stage. In the 1970s, the provocative punk rockers Tedje en de Flikkers and De Heideroosjes were the rage. Next, along came *boerenrock*, sometimes called "farmer's rock," because of its blend of regional dialects in song lyrics. Currently, the

Brothers Rudy (left) and Riem de Wolff led the Blue Diamonds, a popular rock band that had its first hit in 1960. The brothers, shown here in 1986, were known for their harmony. They were born in Indonesia and immigrated to the Netherlands in 1949.

Members of the Dutch national soccer team celebrate a World Cup victory while fans dressed in the team color of orange cheer them on.

indie music scene enlivens Dutch urban nightlife, fueled by fan magazines tracking stars such as Carol van Dijk, lead singer of Bettie Serveert. Bands have developed elaborate Web sites to showcase their heavy beats and rollicking sounds.

Sports

The Dutch always seem to be on the go. They eagerly embrace all sorts of sports and participate in many international competitions.

Football, or soccer, is the most popular sport in the nation. Center forward Johan Cruijff is considered one of the

Fun and Games

Although people in the Netherlands love soccer and other sports that are popular around the world, they also take part in some events that are all their own. *Paalzitten* is a competition where people sit on a platform high on a pole. The winner is the person who stays up there the longest. In *klootschieten*, the players compete to toss a leaded ball as far as it will go. *Fierljeppen* is a Frisian sport in which people vault over a ditch using a long pole.

game's greatest players. He went on to successfully manage the Dutch powerhouse team Ajax.

The Netherlands' powerful national soccer team is always competitive in the World Cup. These hard-fought soccer championships are held every four years and are the world's most watched sporting event. In 2010, the Netherlands reached its third World Cup final but lost in a bruising match to Spain. But in 2014, the Dutch took third place in the competition.

When winter's blustery cold arrives, many Dutch head to the outdoors for skating on just about every frozen surface in the country. Skating originated in the Low Countries back in the Middle Ages, when it was easier to move around on the icy, wind-swept waterways than fight through snowdrifts. Back then, people strapped cow ribs to their feet to use as skates. Cumbersome wooden blocks were also used as skates for a time, until someone came up with the idea of using a steel blade. Today's highly engineered skate styles evolved from those early devices.

Since 1909, the country's top speed skaters have competed in the grueling 124-mile (200 km) Elfstedentocht tour. Racers hope that the weather is not so cold that it's dangerous or so warm that the ice is melting. In either case, the race may not be held. In 1986, when Willem-Alexander was still crown prince, he skated the Elfstedentocht, under the pseudonym W. A. Van Buren. The last race was held in 1997, when conditions were right for it.

Outdoor rinks, called *IJsbanen*, can also be found throughout the country. Amsterdam's Jaap Eden is one of the oldest artificial ice-skating rinks in the world: It celebrated its 50th anniversary in 2011. The rink is also home to the Amstel Tijgers professional ice hockey team.

Some families push baby carriages while ice-skating on the frozen lakes near Loosdrecht, in the central part of the country.

The Silver Skates

One of the most beloved Dutch children's stories is *Hans Brinker, or the Silver Skates*. In 1865, Mary Mapes Dodge (1831–1905) wrote the tale about a Dutch brother and sister, Hans and Gretel, who hope to win a set of silver skates in a race. After overcoming many challenges, Gretel wins the competition.

The Dutch typically make a great showing during Olympic skating events. At the 2014 games, athletes from the Netherlands took eight of the twelve gold medals in long-track speed skating, as well as seven silver and eight bronze. Of thirty-six possible medals overall, the Netherlands captured twenty-three, setting an Olympic record. Top Dutch skaters include Jorrit Bergsma, who took home gold in the 10,000 m race.

Jorrit Bergsma races around the track at the 2014 Winter Olympics.

On the Go

During warmer months, the Dutch pedal their bicycles everywhere. The average Dutch person cycles almost 600 miles (900 km) per year. Many Dutch people have more than one bike: a fancier model for long-distance riding and another with a basket to carry groceries or schoolbooks. There are about sixteen million bicycles in the Netherlands, and about 1.3 million new bicycles are sold every year. Taking advantage of their flat country, the Dutch have built a vast network of cycle paths. They are clearly marked, smoothly surfaced pathways with separate signs and lights for travelers on two wheels. The paths, *fietspaden*, are wide enough to allow side-by-side cycling and passing.

Dutch people bicycle through Utrecht. More than 30 percent of people in the Netherlands say cycling is their main mode of transportation.

Baby bicycle carriages are popular in the Netherlands.

As babies and toddlers, Dutch youngsters travel in special seats on sturdy cargo bikes. These seats are often equipped with canopies to protect the children from the rain or hot sun. Dutch teens use their bikes because it is often easier than taking a car. Cyclists are accommodated in many ways. The Groningen train station has underground parking for ten thousand bikes.

With this emphasis on cycling, Dutch athletes naturally are tough competitors. The Dutch have won more than forty medals in cycling events at the Summer Olympics over the years. In 2013, Dutch cyclist Danny van Poppel raced for the Trek Factory Racing Team, representing one of the world's largest bike manufacturers. At age nineteen, in 2013, he was the youngest competitor since World War II in the Tour de France. Marianne Vos is one of the top Dutch female cyclists.

About 4.5 million Dutch people are registered at a sports club. Many people also enjoy hang gliding, windsurfing, sailing, parachuting, go-karting, wall climbing, or mudflat hiking. Whatever the activity, some Dutch people will want to join in.

Windsurfers battle high waves near large cargo ships in the North Sea.

Champion Horsewoman

Anky van Grunsven is an expert Dutch horse rider, holding nine Olympic medals—the most ever won by an equestrian athlete. Van Grunsven competed in every Olympics between 1988 and 2012, winning a total of three gold medals, five silvers, and one bronze. She is also the only person to compete at seven successive Olympics in dressage, an event in which the horse and rider demonstrate their training by performing a series of precise movements, and the only rider to record three successive Olympic wins in the same event.

CHAPTER 10

Food
and Fun

THE NETHERLANDS IS A WELCOMING LAND. PEOPLE enjoy the bikes paths, the many fragrant flowers, and healthy foods. They also enjoy spending time with their friends and family. Even after they grow up, many people continue to live near their parents.

Opposite: **A Dutch family in winter. The average family in the Netherlands has one or two children.**

Let's Eat

Dutch cuisine is a mix of world flavors. In addition to traditional Dutch fare, it includes influences from China, Indonesia, Suriname, Turkey, Morocco, and other cultures. *Stamppot* is a hearty winter dish made with mashed potatoes, kale or carrots, and sausage. *Snert* is a thick pea soup served with smoked bacon on a hearty chunk of rye bread. *Bami goreng* is of Indonesian origin, made with a stir-fried egg, peppers, onions, meat, and lots of garlic. Slim white asparagus, herring, French fries with slathers of mayonnaise, and meat croquettes are also popular. The Dutch are avid milk consumers. They also love their cheese, eating about 46 pounds (21 kg) each year.

The typical Dutch family eats three meals a day. In the morning, Dutch children often devour sandwiches made with

A grandmother joins her family for breakfast.

cheese or peanut butter. Lunch is simple, often sandwiches made with thinly sliced smoked sausage called *rookworst*, and a small salad. Dinner is served around 6:00 p.m. It is usually a three-course meal starting with soup. The main dish is often a mix of potatoes with vegetables and some kind of meat, fish, or chicken. Kids also love *frikandel*, which is like a minced-meat hot dog. Desserts are always popular and consist of apple-filled crèpes, Limburg raisin cake, or small spongy pancakes called *poffertjes*.

Bread is served at almost every meal in the Netherlands, often with thin pieces of cheese sliced by a special wide-blade knife called a *kaasschaaf*. Every day in the Netherlands, more than 750,000 slices of bread are eaten with *hagelslag*, a topping made of chocolate or colored sugar sprinkles.

Poffertjes

Poffertjes are small, delicious pancake puff treats that are often sold from stands on the street. Have an adult help you with this recipe.

Ingredients

1 teaspoon instant yeast

1 tablespoon milk

1 cup buckwheat flour

1 cup flour

2 eggs

1 teaspoon sugar

½ teaspoon salt

1 ¼ cups warm milk

1 tablespoon butter

Directions

In a small bowl, dissolve the yeast in 1 tablespoon of milk. In a separate bowl, combine the buckwheat flour, flour, eggs, sugar, salt, and half the milk. Add the dissolved yeast from the first bowl. Whisk until smooth. Add the remaining milk and beat again. Cover the bowl with plastic wrap and let it sit for an hour.

Melt the butter in a frying pan. When it sizzles, add the batter in 1 teaspoon amounts in circular movements to create the mini pancakes. Using two forks, turn the poffertjes over as soon as the bottom has set. Cook until brown.

Serve the pancake puffs with butter and powdered sugar. Enjoy!

Many Dutch people have a passion for sweets. They do not need an excuse to gobble down *oliebollen*, a traditional New Year's Eve treat. These are deep-fried balls of dough, often with raisins or currants. Oliebollen are usually served hot and sprinkled with powdered sugar. Another treat is *Limburgse vlaai*, a pie with a tasty light crust packed with cherries, plums, or apricots. Dutch candy includes *chocoladeletters*, chocolate made into the form of a letter and served around Saint Nicholas Day.

A baker makes oliebollen, which are sometimes called Dutch doughnuts.

The Dutch are among the world's biggest coffee drinkers, consuming an average of 3.2 cups a day, which works out to 36 gallons (136 liters) of coffee every year. Coffee plays a major role in people's social lives and is part of being a good friend and neighbor. Neighbors often invite each other over for a cup. This custom is called *gezelligheid* (time spent with loved ones). A popular variety of coffee is *koffie verkeerd*, the Dutch version of a caffè latte. This is a cup of hot coffee or espresso, stirred with a lot of steamed milk and an added sugar cube.

Friends take a coffee break at a café. The average Dutch person drinks more than twice as much coffee as the average American.

The Dutch also enjoy beer, with the average adult drinking about 19 gallons (72 l) a year. The Dutch brewery Heineken is the third-largest brewer in the world.

What to Wear

No one wears traditional Dutch clothing anymore, except at shows for tourists or on special holidays. But centuries ago, Dutch men wore baggy pants and shirts, while women wore perky bonnets and flared skirts. These days, many Dutch are fashionable dressers. Some wear business suits and the latest styles while others prefer jeans and T-shirts.

Time to Relax

The Dutch love eating out and dropping in at coffee bars and casual cafés. Cities are filled with clubs where young people go to dance, listen to music, and snack from night until early morning.

The Dutch enjoy being tourists in their own country. Each July thousands of Dutch schoolchildren and their

Boats crowd the canals of Amsterdam on King's Day, a holiday celebrating the king's birthday. Many people wear orange on this day because the Dutch royal family belongs to the House of Orange.

parents stroll through the streets in crowded parades called the *avondvierdaagse*, or Four-Days Marches. During their walks, as they enjoy the sights, they eat half-cut lemons and sweets tied on strings that they wear around their necks. This tradition started in 1909 to promote sport and exercise. Children also enjoy visiting Madurodam in The Hague. This is a park that showcases miniature replicas of Dutch landmarks and

National Holidays

New Year's Day	January 1
Good Friday	March or April
Easter Sunday	March or April
Easter Monday	March or April
King's Birthday	April 26
National Liberation Day	May 5
Whitsuntide	May or June
Ascension Day	May or June
Christmas	December 25 and 26

historical cities. Another favorite stop is the Euromast, an observation tower in Rotterdam that rises 341 feet (104 m) high, providing an expansive view of the city far below. For Dutch people and visitors alike, the Netherlands is a great place to explore.

Hello, Saint Nicholas

Dutch children look forward to Saint Nicholas Day, which is celebrated on December 6. The night before, presents are tucked into kids' shoes or hidden under their beds. The celebration starts in late November when Saint Nicholas and his sidekick, Black Peter, sail into the Rotterdam harbor. From there, they parade through the brightly decorated city. The real Saint Nicholas is thought to have originated in the fourth century in the Middle East. He may have been the Bishop of Myra, in Turkey. The depiction of Black Peter is controversial, and many Dutch now object to this character. They believe it is demeaning to black people.

Timeline

DUTCH HISTORY

People from central Europe begin migrating into what is now the Netherlands.	**ca. 4500** BCE
Celts and Teutons migrate to the Netherlands.	**ca. 300** BCE
Romans invade the Low Countries.	**57** BCE
The Vikings raid the region.	**800s–early 1000s**
The first dikes are constructed in the Netherlands.	**1100s**
The Hanseatic League gains power.	**1100s–1200s**
The Low Countries become part of the Habsburg Empire.	**1477**
Dutch rebels begin the Eighty Years' War against Spain.	**1568**
Pacification of Ghent is signed, establishing religious tolerance.	**1576**
The Dutch East India Company is founded.	**1602**
The Dutch establish colonies around the world.	**Early to mid-1600s**

WORLD HISTORY

ca. 2500 BCE	The Egyptians build the pyramids and the Sphinx in Giza.
ca. 563 BCE	The Buddha is born in India.
313 CE	The Roman emperor Constantine legalizes Christianity.
610	The Prophet Muhammad begins preaching a new religion called Islam.
1054	The Eastern (Orthodox) and Western (Roman Catholic) Churches break apart.
1095	The Crusades begin.
1215	King John seals the Magna Carta.
1300s	The Renaissance begins in Italy.
1347	The plague sweeps through Europe.
1453	Ottoman Turks capture Constantinople, conquering the Byzantine Empire.
1492	Columbus arrives in North America.
1500s	Reformers break away from the Catholic Church, and Protestantism is born.

DUTCH HISTORY

Spain recognizes the Netherlands' independence in the Peace of Westphalia. **1648**

The Kingdom of Holland is annexed to France. **1810**

The Netherlands regains its independence. **1815**

The Royal Dutch Petroleum Company is founded. **1890**

The Netherlands remains neutral as World War I starts. **1914**

Germany invades the Netherlands. **1940**

The Netherlands grants Indonesia its independence. **1949**

The Netherlands becomes a founding member of the European Economic Community. **1957**

Netherlands grants independence to Suriname. **1975**

The Dutch parliament ratifies the Maastricht Treaty, establishing the European Union. **1992**

Severe flooding causes the evacuation of 250,000 people and $1 billion in damage. **1995**

The Netherlands becomes the first nation in the world to legalize same sex marriage. **2001**

Willem-Alexander becomes king. **2013**

WORLD HISTORY

1776 The U.S. Declaration of Independence is signed.

1789 The French Revolution begins.

1865 The American Civil War ends.

1879 The first practical lightbulb is invented.

1914 World War I begins.

1917 The Bolshevik Revolution brings communism to Russia.

1929 A worldwide economic depression begins.

1939 World War II begins.

1945 World War II ends.

1969 Humans land on the Moon.

1975 The Vietnam War ends.

1989 The Berlin Wall is torn down as communism crumbles in Eastern Europe.

1991 The Soviet Union breaks into separate states.

2001 Terrorists attack the World Trade Center in New York City and the Pentagon near Washington, D.C.

2004 A tsunami in the Indian Ocean destroys coastlines in Africa, India, and Southeast Asia.

2008 The United States elects its first African American president.

Fast Facts

Official name:	Kingdom of the Netherlands
Capital:	Amsterdam
Seat of government:	The Hague
Official language:	Dutch

Amsterdam

NETHERLANDS
- Cities of more than 220,000 people
- Other cities
- National capital

0   40 miles
0   40 kilometers

North Sea

Waddenzee

Den Helder

Dokkum
Leeuwarden
Harlingen
Sneek
Heerenveen
Eastermar
Drachten
Veendam
Delfzijl
Groningen
Assen
Stadskanaal
Wolvega

Andijk
Hoorn
Steenwijk
Emmeloord
Meppel
Emmen
Hoogeveen
Hardenberg

Alkmaar
Edam
Lelystad
Dronten
Kampen
Zwolle
IJmuiden
Biddinghuizen
Almelo
Oldenzaal
Haarlem
Almere
Harderwijk
Rijssen
Hengelo
Enschede
Zuid-Kennemerland National Park
Amsterdam (constitutional capital)
Deventer
Apeldoorn

The Hague (seat of government)
Leiden
Woerden
Amersfoort
Barneveld
Hoge Veluwe National Park
Zutphen
Winterswijk
Utrecht
Zoetermeer
Gouda
Veenendaal
Arnhem
Doetinchem
Schiedam
Rotterdam
Tiel
Nijmegen
Hellevoetsluis
Gorinchem
Derdrecht
Middelharnis
Oss
's-Hertogenbosch
Oosterhout
Roosendaal
Breda
Tilburg
Helmond
Middelburg
Goes
Bergen op Zoom
Eindhoven
Venlo
Terneuzen
Weert
Roermond
Maastricht

IJsselmeer
Holland

Rhine R.
Maas R.

BELGIUM

GERMANY

Netherlands

National flag

Official religion:	None
Year of Founding:	1579
Founder:	William of Orange
National anthem:	"Het Wilhelmus" ("The William")
Government:	Constitutional monarchy
Head of state:	Monarch
Head of government:	Prime minister
Area:	16,033 square miles (41,525 sq km)
Longitude and latitude of geographic center:	52°30' N, 5°45' E
Bordering countries:	Germany to the east and Belgium to the south
Highest elevation:	Vaalserberg, 1,053 (321 m) above sea level
Lowest elevation:	Prins Alexanderpolder, 22 feet (7 m) below sea level
Average daily high temperature:	In Amsterdam, 42°F (6°C) in January, 72°F (22°C) in July
Average daily low temperature:	In Amsterdam, 33°F (1°C) in January, 54°F (12°C) in July
Average annual rainfall:	33 inches (84 cm)

Coastline

Binnenhof

Currency

National population (2013 est.): 16,779,575

Population of major cities (2014 est.):

Amsterdam	810,937
Rotterdam	618,357
The Hague	508,940
Utrecht	328,164
Eindhoven	220,920

Landmarks:
- ▶ *Anne Frank House*, Amsterdam
- ▶ *Binnenhof*, The Hague
- ▶ *Dom Tower*, Utrecht
- ▶ *Euromast*, Rotterdam
- ▶ *Keukenhof National Park*, South Holland

Economy: The Netherlands has a thriving, well-developed economy. For centuries, it has been a center of international trade, and today it is one of the top ten exporting countries in the world. Tourism is big business in the Netherlands, where more than 14 million foreign visitors arrive each year. Oil is refined in the Netherlands, and Royal Dutch Shell, the second-largest oil company is based there. Food products, metals, chemicals, and machinery are all manufactured in the Netherlands. Major agricultural products grown in the country include flowers, potatoes, and tomatoes. The country also produces high quality dairy products such as milk and cheese.

Currency: The euro. In 2015, 1 euro equaled US$1.12, and US$1.00 equaled 89 euros.

System of weights and measures: Metric system

Literacy rate (2014): 99%

Classroom

Benedict de Spinoza

Common Dutch words and phrases:

goedemorgen	good morning
goedenacht	good night
alstublieft	please
dank u wel	thank you
Welkom!	Welcome!
Tot ziens!	See you later!

Prominent Dutch people:

Desiderius Erasmus (1466–1536)
Philosopher

Rembrandt van Rijn (1606–1669)
Painter

Benedict de Spinoza (1632–1677)
Philosopher

Vincent van Gogh (1853–1890)
Painter

Marianne Vos (1987–)
Bicycling champion

Willem-Alexander (1967–)
King

William I of Orange (1533–1584)
Founder of the Dutch Republic

To Find Out More

Books

► Altman, Linda Jacobs, *Hidden Teens, Hidden Lives: Primary Sources from the Holocaust.* Berkeley Heights, NJ: Enslow Publishers, 2010.

► Crispino, Enrica. *Van Gogh.* Minneapolis: Oliver Press, 2008.

► Goossens, Jesse, and Charlotte Dematons. *Holland/1000 Things About Holland.* Smyrna, TN: Lemniscaat USA, 2013.

Video

► *Anne Frank Remembered.* New York: Sony Pictures Classics, 2010.

► *Van Gogh: Brush with Genius.* Chatsworth, CA: Image Entertainment, 2010.

▶ Visit this Scholastic Web site for more information on the Netherlands:
www.factsfornow.scholastic.com
Enter the keyword **Netherlands**

Index

Page numbers in *italics* indicate illustrations.

Meet the Author

MARTIN HINTZ IS A FORMER newspaper reporter and editor. He has contributed more than forty books to Scholastic Publishing's Enchantment of the World series, as well as titles in the America the Beautiful series. He has traveled throughout the world researching stories for books and articles and is a past president of the Society of American Travel Writers. Hintz is also the publisher of the Irish American Post, a news outlet covering Irish and Irish American culture, sports, entertainment, business, and politics.

Hintz and his wife, Pam, operate a farm near Milwaukee, Wisconsin, where they grow vegetables and raise rabbits, turkeys, goats, and pigs. The couple has written books and articles about cheese, farm life, chickens, and other agricultural subjects.

Photo Credits